Mini-Wife Syndrome:
A Stepmother's Guide

Katie Lee Douglas

CONTENTS

Mini-Wife Syndrome:
A Stepmother's Guide

By: Katie Lee Douglas

INTRODUCTION

A familiar sense of dread settled in my gut as we made the short trip to pick up my eleven year old stepdaughter for "our" weekend.

"What do you want to do for dinner?" I ask my husband, Big D, a bit listlessly.

"I dunno," he says, pointing at a little local diner as we pass, "do you want to go to the Roadside Grill?"

I glance up and shake my head, "Nah… the last few times we've been there I didn't care for the food. How about Burger King?"

He shakes his head. "Shell doesn't like Burger King."

Shell doesn't like much of anything, but I didn't say that out loud. "Okay, well, maybe we should just pick up some hot dogs and eat at home."

"Sounds good to me," he says.

Shell is always late coming out of her mom's house,

which leaves us sitting awkwardly in the driveway.

Oftentimes, it gives Shell's birth mother, hereinafter referred to as BM, an excuse to come out and chit chat with my husband, laying her hands all over him, laughing with him over the antics and accomplishments of "their" child. Big D professes to hate talking to BM. I tend to believe that if he really hated talking to her, he would say something to Shell about being on time.

Shell opens the door and jumps into the truck in an action more suited to a five year old than a preteen.

"Hi Daddyyyy," she says.

"Hey, Baby," he says. He doesn't ever seem to notice that she rarely acknowledges me. We pull out of the driveway into the road. Looking over his shoulder he says, "Would you like to go to Roadside Grill or go home and have hot dogs?"

"Roadside Grill!" she yells in the excited voice of a preschooler.

I bite my tongue. Hard. Didn't he and I just have this conversation? But as usual, I say nothing, and seconds later we pull into the Roadside Grill.

I look around the familiar diner where just about a year and a half before, my husband and I had come for our first impromptu date. I like the little diner and the memories it holds. I just don't like the food very much.

Shell slides into one side of a booth. I slide into the other, leaving Big D to choose his seat. He chooses to sit next to Shell, as usual.

Usually I am pretty good at ignoring these sorts of things, but tonight something was malfunctioning. My head started to ache and my insides literally hurt as I ordered a grilled cheese and French fries and sat awkwardly in the center of my booth seat while my husband and his daughter cuddled and giggled on the other side.

Big D kept his arm around Shell while we waited for what seemed like eternity on our food, and she literally leaned against his chest, looking up into his eyes to giggle just like a teenage lover. Every now and again, Big D would look up at me with that silly "ain't she cute?" look on his face, and then the grin would fall off his face and be replaced with confusion. "What's wrong, Katie?" he asked several times.

"I have a headache," I told him. "I don't feel well."

"You seem like you're mad," he said.

"I'm fine," I insisted, trying to squelch the anger that threatened to consume me.
Shell ordered teriyaki wings and proceeded to eat them like a toddler, getting teriyaki sauce all over her face. Big D literally took a napkin and wiped his preteen's face, looking at me with that stupid grin as he did it. It

almost took an act of congress to keep my eyebrows from rising into my hair.

At this point, I could feel myself slipping. I did not WANT to hurt my husband's feelings by letting him know his daughter was anything but beloved by me, but quite honestly, I couldn't stand to be around her anymore. I was literally sick with dread when "our" Friday came and we had to pick her up for the weekend, and I was ecstatic when Sunday rolled around. I just couldn't keep going like that.

I knew I had to have help.

When we got home, I desperately searched the internet. To my great surprise and no small amount of relief, I found the World Wide Web slap full of complaints from stepmothers like me. Turned out I was not just a horrible, jealous, wicked stepmother, after all. I was a normal female having very normal negative feelings against another female who threatened to take my rightful place in my man's life.

Turned out I had a Mini-Wife on my hands, and I had no earthly idea what to do about it.

Since that night, I have come a long way toward containing and controlling this thing I now call Mini-Wife Syndrome. I will not lie to you and tell you it is totally vanquished. I don't think this is an acute "curable" syndrome. I think stepmothers would do better to look at it as a chronic disease, one they might always have to live with but can control and make bearable with the right treatment.

In this book we are going to talk about some of the things a stepmother can do to recognize and control Mini-Wife Syndrome.

SYMPTOMS OF MINI-WIFE SYNDROME

First of all, in order to control Mini-Wife Syndrome, one must first recognize they actually have a Mini-Wife in their marriage. This is no easy feat. Society has programmed us stepmothers to feel like any problem we have with our stepchildren is always our faults... if we have any negative feelings towards our stepchildren, we have somehow morphed from decent, caring human beings into the horrid, wicked stepmothers portrayed in our childhood fairy tales. Nobody wants to grow up to be wicked. Deep down we know we *aren't* wicked, yet still we doubt ourselves.

Dear stepmother let me lay these doubts to rest for you. If you feel **awkward and excluded** when you spend time with your darling husband and his less-than-darling daughter, then there is probably a very good reason for it. Let me repeat. If your gut tells you something is not right, then something is definitely awry.

Still doubt yourself? Then read on.

The following few paragraphs are a few of the traits I have identified in Shell and have learned from other stepmothers in similar situations that might help you verify that you do, indeed, have a Mini-Wife in your family.

Mini-Wives tend to occur more frequently, and perhaps be more pronounced in relationships where the father has been single for a long period of time. Not always, mind you, but in many situations, including my own, the Mini-Wife's parents divorced several years ago and the father has had few, if any, serious relationships since then. In my case, Big D made it a point not to bring his dates around Shell unless he was serious about them. Since Big D was a confirmed bachelor with zero plans to remarry, suffice it to say that not very many women ever made it to that point. In fact, she had only been introduced to one other woman besides me, and that was several years before me. Since Shell had unfettered, unbridled access to her father at all times, she became accustomed to his sole attention and resources.

Since Mini-Wives are accustomed to the sole attention of their fathers, if there comes a time when she is NOT the center of his attention, she might punish him by pouting, whining, or ignoring him. In fact, many of these girls seem to not be able to entertain themselves at all. If they aren't the center of their father's attention, they will have a long, sad face.

Or they will do something to cause themselves to become the center of attention, even if that involves misbehaving. For the Mini-Wife, negative attention from Daddy is better than no attention at all.

The Mini-Wife may be overly affectionate towards her father, and might even be inappropriate in her affections. As mentioned before, my stepdaughter used to feel like she must be sitting next to Daddyyy at all times, holding his hand, kissing him several times an hour, etc. Recently she has started moving up behind him and pressing herself lengthwise against his body like a wife would do with her husband. And when she hugs him, she doesn't want to let him go despite him trying to move away from her. I have read of Mini-Wives who want to "spoon" with their fathers and/or cuddle under blankets while watching television, or worse, Mini-Wives who still insist on sleeping in the same bed with their fathers, even as teenagers.

When we go out in public, my husband and I have a hard time walking like normal people. Why? Because Shell is constantly maneuvering to place herself between my husband and me. She prefers to walk hand-in-hand, or worse, arm-in-arm with him, leaving me to straggle along behind them like a child. During our first year together, this used to happen *a lot*, and it felt awkward and exclusive and just plain wrong. Suffice it to say that in our relationship, Katie Lee no longer follows along like a lost child, and Big D is fully aware.

The Mini-Wife may become angry or hurt with her father for showing physical affection to her stepmother. I have become accustomed to hearing the loud sighs and tongue clicks that occur whenever Big D and I spend any amount of time in each other's arms, or Heaven Forbid, kissing. Many stepmothers report Mini-Wives actually pushing themselves between Dad and his wife or verbally insisting they do not show physical affection for one another in the Mini-Wife's presence. One Mini-Wife even insisted her father and stepmother refrain from having sex in the same house as she. And I've ceased to be surprised at how many of these guilty dads actually obey their daughter's commands!

The Mini-Wife might seem obsessed with her father. For instance, she might call him several times a day, or insist on speaking with him on the phone while he's out, especially if she knows he's with her stepmother. My stepdaughter's Facebook profile picture is one with herself cheek to cheek with her father. Her Instagram profile lists "Hanging with Dad" as her hobby. She even tells me she has "fantasies" of herself and her father sitting together in a deer stand...?

The Mini-Wife insists on private dates with Dad. And this is a trap that many dads and stepmothers fall into. The mini-wife whines and complains she doesn't get enough "daddy-daughter" time, and even though it kills her soul, the stepmother backs off and allows it in an effort to prove she's not so wicked after all. However, this well-meaning effort only serves to give the mini-wife more reason to believe she has equal status with her stepmother.

The Mini-Wife feels she has equal standing with her stepmother. If darling husband brings home flowers for his wife, Heaven forbid he forgets to bring a bouquet for his Mini-Wife. If he kisses his wife, Mini-Wife expects one, as well. If he takes his wife on a special date, then Princess must go on a special date, too. Some Mini-Wives even expect to take turns in the front seat of the car, or expect Daddy to alternate sitting next to them and their stepmother at the restaurant.

A stepmother living with a Mini-Wife might begin to feel she is in a polygamist marriage that she did not sign up for. The Mini-Wife might feel it is okay to "tattle" to Daddyyy on her stepmother, she might be involved in decisions that *should not* include a child, or she might feel she has (or actually does have) as much or more influence over Daddyyy as her stepmother.

The Mini-Wife cherishes past memories or the time before stepmother was in the picture. And she brings them up liberally. "Daddyyy, remember that time we blah, blah, blah…" Constantly. It's enough to send a stepmother to her room to hide. The purpose of this, of course, is to have an exclusive moment with

Daddy that cannot possibly include the stepmother who cannot participate in the memory. It also serves to remind the stepmother that she came AFTER the Mini-Wife and somehow that gives her less stature in the triangle.

The Mini-Wife speaks in a "babyish" voice and engages in "helpless" or "Damsel in Distress" behavior. The word "Daddyyyyy," coming from an almost teenage girl can certainly raise eyebrows. I have never been so speechless in all my life as when my twelve year old stepdaughter, sitting in a public restaurant, mind you, intoned in a six-year-old voice to my dear husband, "Daddyyyyy….can you cut up my pancake?" AND HE DID IT!!! I seriously thought I was going to faint. And the "Damsel in Distress" behavior? Shell is a master at it. I wish I had a dime for every time Shell has "fallen" and "injured" herself so badly she needed Daddyyyy to hold her and dry her tears. Or protect her from all those big bad bullies who so often "pick on her."

The Mini-Wife feels like she is the Woman of the House. Or at least as much the Woman of the House as her stepmother. Once, when I first married my darling husband, I packed away some dolphins from the shelf and replaced them with the décor of my choice. Shell threw a fit. You'd have thought I'd torn the house down. Turns out she and my husband had picked those dolphins out together and I was an evil wicked stepmother for daring to move them. Mini-Wife stepdaughters may feel it is completely acceptable to verbalize their opinions on most everything that goes on in their households, and become upset when their opinions are not honored.

Mini-Wives try to "take care" of Daddy. My stepdaughter is always on the alert for any little thing she can do for her father. Daddyyyy, do you need another drink? Do you want me to get your jacket? Fix your plate? Rub your feet? This is just another way the Mini-Wife might compete with her stepmother to convince herself and others that she is actually the "true wife" in the home.

Mini-Wives jump at any chance to side with Daddy against their stepmother. Even if your husband is just joking around with you, anything that can possibly be perceived as a divide between the two of you will find Mini-Wife jumping on Daddy's bandwagon to team up against stepmother. Daddy doesn't like the pork chops? Neither does Mini-Wife. In fact, she thought they were horrible and Stepmother is terribly wicked to have served such fare. Daddy mentions he is out of clean socks? Mini-Wife has suffered horribly about that very same issue!

Mini-Wives believe they are special, and therefore entitled to special treatment. Because they have long been the sole recipient of their fathers' attention and affection, and often have guilty-dads who tend to give in to their every wish, Mini-Wives tend to have Princess Attitudes. They feel they should have the first choice of everything from which seat they will occupy to which portion of cake they'd like reserved for themselves. Conversation must revolve around them, and everyone is expected to be acutely interested in every word that drops from their royal mouths.

Of course, the girl with the Princess Attitude does not usually win any popularity contests. On the contrary, the young mini-wife is often lonely and friendless, or worse, the mean girl other children avoid. This, of course, makes her guilty fathers even more distraught that his princess is unhappy so he caters to her wishes even more than ever, often leaving the Mini-Wife to conclude that she is mistreated and misunderstood simply because she's special and no one but Daddy seems to recognize it.

ETIOLOGY OF MINI-WIFE SYNDROME

In order to control Mini-Wife Syndrome, it is helpful to try to understand some of its root causes. I am not a psychology major, but I took a few child psychology classes during my college years and made some observations while raising children of my own. With that foundation and some independent research, I have a few theories about how some of this ludicrous behavior begins and how it is nurtured to become the disease Mini-Wife Syndrome truly is.

Electra Complex

When my daughter was three years old, she became seriously attached to her biological father, to whom I was still married at the time. Even though she had always been a "Mama's girl" to that point, this new behavior didn't concern me because I recognized it as perfectly natural female development.

It is normal, and even desirable, for little girls to become strongly attracted to their fathers during their preschool years. Their father is and should be their "first love." Some little girls might even verbalize their wish to marry their father when they grow up. This stage of development is very important for little girls to experience because they are learning gender development. Sigmund Freud called this stage *Reverse Oedipus Complex* but later psychologists have termed it the *Electra Complex*.

During this time, the little girl might try very hard to replace her mother in her father's affections, but as the marriage progresses unaffected, she gradually arrives at the conclusion that she is unable to compete with the much older, wiser woman in her father's life. At this point, a healthy little girl will give up the competition with her mother and, instead, identify with her and try to emulate her so that one day the little girl can grow up and win the love and affection of her very own prince.

In certain cases of Mini-Wife Syndrome, I believe the little girl *never learns* she cannot compete with her mother for her father's highest affections. Perhaps her parents divorced too early for this process to occur or the marriage was too rocky for her to see the affection and devotion between her parents? Or perhaps she even had a stepmother present in her life but still never learned the needed lesson because she was *permitted* to successfully compete with her stepmother due to Dad's guilty conscience and his consequent refusal to set needed boundaries. For whatever reason, she never fully came to the conclusion she could not be "the woman" in her father's life.

One of the main goals a stepmother might have in learning to control Mini-Wife Syndrome is teaching the Mini-Wife that she cannot (or can no longer) compete with her stepmother. It would be very helpful to have Dad's help with this, but unfortunately, Dad is often just as blind to the problem as the Mini-Wife. In later chapters we will discuss some of the things a stepmother can do on her own to teach her stepdaughter her proper role in the family, as well as some things she can say to her husband to help him realize that Mini-Wife Syndrome is unhealthy both for his daughter and his marriage.

Guilty Dad Syndrome

Guilt is just a normal part of parenting, but the normal guilt of a parent seems to be multiplied a thousand times in fathers who have failed in their marriages. Because they were unable to make their relationships work, they tend to feel an obligation to "make it up" to their children in any possible way they can. Whereas a father still married to her mother would have no problem recognizing what is appropriate in his daughter and what is not, the guilt that fathers seem to harbor after a divorce can be a major factor in keeping a dad from teaching his daughter proper boundaries.

Whereas a non-divorced father might begin discouraging his seven year old daughter from sitting on his lap, a divorced dad might still be allowing his daughter to sit on his lap at age sixteen. And even though a man in an intact marriage might insist his child learn to sleep in her own bed by the age of three or four, a divorced dad might find himself still sharing a bed with his twelve year old daughter.

"Why?" we stepmothers want to know. "Why does this seemingly strong, masculine man I married turn into such a lily-livered pansy when dealing with his daughter?" The answer might simply be that he cannot bring himself to cause his offspring anymore pain than he already caused by his failure in the marriage. In learning to control Mini-Wife Syndrome, a stepmother might first need to help her husband see that he has been parenting from guilt rather than good common sense and this is not an effective way to bring up a child.

Human Nature Abhors a Vacuum

As I mentioned before, many of these Mini-Wives are formed when their fathers are divorced for long periods of time. As we were all taught in elementary school that "Nature Abhors a Vacuum," so does *human nature* abhor a vacuum. Since the position of wife appears to be open beside a divorced man, it can easily suck a young female right on in.

The seat beside Dad is empty so his daughter fills it. She is his dinner date. She accompanies him to the movies, to the County Fair, even to his hair appointment. She assists him when he fixes stuff around the house. She helps him choose the curtains, their brand of toothpaste, what they will have for dinner. He is lonely so he talks to her. She is the sole recipient of all his attention and affection. She is scared at night and there is room in his double bed for her to sleep with him. Even though this is a completely non-sexual relationship, for all other intents and purposes, she is his partner in life. In effect, she is his Mini-Wife, and she rarely takes it well when another woman comes along.

A stepmother who intends to control Mini-Wife Syndrome must learn to hold and protect her position as Queen of the Castle. The seat next to her darling husband, the King, belongs to none other than his Queen. All decisions related to the running of the Castle are approved by the Queen. The Queen owns the sole right to sleep beside the King. Only the Queen goes on special outings with the King. You get the picture, dear stepmother. Only when you recognize your right and position as Queen will you have the confidence to take your place beside your husband and banish Mini-Wife Syndrome from your Castle.

Emotional Incest

In the world of psychology, some cases of Mini-Wife Syndrome are more accurately called Emotional Incest. In its simpler form, Emotional Incest occurs when an adult uses a child to fill a void in his or her life that should be reserved for another adult. Most of the time, the divorced father has no idea he is even doing this, let alone that it can be harmful to his daughter.

Yet from Passive-Aggressive behavior to extreme Narcissism, the harmful effects of Emotional Incest are well-documented, the severity depending very much on the level the child has been allowed to immerse herself into the "adult" role.

Sometimes the mere term "Emotional Incest" grabs a father's attention when his new wife or significant other is trying to talk to him about Mini-Wife Syndrome. (However, be quick to assure him you are not talking about any kind of sexual relationship or misconduct.) Most men are not even aware that Emotional Incest exists. They feel they are simply being a good father by putting so much of themselves into the relationship. A stepmother might explain to such a father that his child is not equipped emotionally to handle adult problems and/or be an emotional support for an adult. Even though the Mini-Wife might appear to be handling the relationship well, even enjoying it, it can cause her problems with normal personality development, as well as current and future relationships.

COMPLICATIONS OF
MINI-WIFE SYNDROME

Like any disease, Mini-Wife Syndrome comes with its own unique set of complications, not only for the Mini-Wife herself, but for the husband, the wife, and their marriage. The following are a few of these complications that can be helpful for a wife to recognize in order for her to learn to control Mini-Wife Syndrome. We will discuss in a later chapter how the couple together, as well as the stepmother alone, might help minimize these complications.

Mini-Wives become acutely unhappy when their father becomes interested in another woman. Since much of their self-esteem and feelings of being "special" are tied up in being their father's Mini-Wife, they tend to resent their new stepmother and feel their father no longer loves them. Even now, years into my relationship with her father, my stepdaughter still struggles with sharing her father with me. Just a few days ago, she threw herself on the floor and cried to her father, "I'm just not used to having anybody else around! It is supposed to be just me and you!" Shell has told me several times she doesn't feel like she will be happy again until "things are back the way they used to be." No matter how many times we talk to her about change and how it has brought about many good things into her life, she still has difficulty accepting that another woman has importance in her father's life.

Fathers of Mini-Wives have problems in relationships with women. When I first met my husband, he was very reluctant to introduce me to Shell. We literally almost broke up before our relationship ever got started simply because every other weekend was reserved for Shell, and I wasn't allowed to meet her. That should have been a warning to me, but fortunately (for him, at least) he realized he was losing me and made the introduction.

I am told by friends that the one other serious relationship he had with a woman in the seven years since his divorce ended because of Shell.
Big D didn't realize what the problem was, but it didn't take me long to figure it out, as I'm sure every woman he was ever interested in before me discovered... the

position of Wife was already occupied in his heart. I have never met a woman who wants to meet the man of her dreams and be his, um, #2...?... woman for eternity. Have you?

Stepmothers feel they are living with the "other woman." Whenever I leave the room, Shell very often jumps into my seat next to her father. When I return, she only stares at me until my husband remembers to ask her to move. I have walked into a room many times to see their heads close together in intimate conversation, only to break apart guiltily when they become aware of my presence. And oftentimes, Shell will look at me with the snotty, superior look of the "other woman" when she is engaging my husband in a deep, intimate hug.

I find myself being literally afraid to leave Big D alone with his daughter, because inevitably, when I return I find she has convinced him to do something (or allow her to do something) that I disagree with, often vehemently. Life becomes a constant power struggle when you live with the other woman in your home, because as a rule, your opinion is the polar opposite of hers.

Stepmothers feel there's "something missing" in their relationships with their husbands. And they are right. If a husband already has a "best friend," a "life confidante," or basically a "life partner," they have no business getting married. No wonder second marriages have up to a 75% chance of ending in divorce where stepchildren are concerned.

Mini-Wives grow up to have problems with their own relationships. After all, where is she to find someone who will treat her as well as her father? Fathers are (supposedly) mature, grown men with an instinct toward protecting and caring for their daughters. When they are cast in the wrong role in their daughter's minds, it stands to reason that no man her age can compete.

First of all, her young man of interest does not have that inner desire to see Daddy's Princess happy above all else, especially at first. He is probably not willing to put up with her whining and excessive thirst for attention for very long. Quite possibly she won't get past the first couple of dates with him. Why? Because no one likes a narcissist, and that's exactly what these Mini-Wives tend to become.

This is perhaps the scariest complication of all. Because what stepmother doesn't long for the day when her Mini-Wife stepdaughter will find a boyfriend of her own and no longer be interested in causing problems in her father's marriage? Unfortunately, we cannot depend on Princess to find her prince unless it becomes apparent to her that there is a new woman in the castle, and she is the QUEEN.

GOALS FOR MANAGING
MINI-WIFE SYNDROME

In order to effectively control Mini-Wife Syndrome, there are several goals the family with a Mini-Wife has to achieve:

The Mini-Wife needs to understand and accept that she cannot compete with her stepmother. Just as a 3-5 year old would learn during the Electra Complex stage of her development that she cannot compete with her mother, the Mini-Wife needs to learn the same with her stepmother in order to proceed with healthy emotional development.

Dad needs to recognize and deal with Guilty Dad Syndrome. Just as Mini-Wife Syndrome is a chronic disease, so is Guilty Dad Syndrome (to be dealt with in another book). Our plan for achieving this goal is two-fold and involves educating dad on the terrible effects of parenting from guilt, and preventing even more guilt that might come from feeling his princess is being mistreated.

Close any "hole" or vacant position in Dad's life other than the Office of Daughter. The Office of Wife is filled. The sooner the Mini-Wife recognizes and accepts this, the better off the family will be.

Any Emotional Incest must cease immediately. Again, this comes down to recognizing what is appropriate for the Office of Wife and what is appropriate for the Office of Daughter. If Emotional Incest is deep-seated and has gone on too long, the family might consider seeing a professional counselor; however, in most cases it is a matter of adjusting habits and behaviors to better suit the roles of each member in the family.

TREATMENTS AND REMEDIES FOR MINI-WIFE SYNDROME

With the previous goals in mind, we are going to go into some of the things we can do to learn to control Mini-Wife Syndrome. Some of the things I am going to suggest might sound cruel or mean. Some of them are going to sound manipulative. The key is to remember the goals.

Re-read them if you must. But essentially they are this: *To teach the Mini-Wife she cannot be the Wife, and do this with the least amount of guilt and upset to your husband.*

Change is never easy and the Mini-Wife has to do the most changing of all. It will not be pleasant. But pitying and babying the Mini-Wife is not the answer. (Remember, she's been pitied and babied much of her life and it has created the disease you are trying to deal with now.)

So put away your guilt, dear stepmother, and do the hard work that needs to be done to make changes in your household that might save your sanity and marriage.

Becoming Your Husband's Number One Priority

Single dads have been programmed to believe that their children must be the number one priority in their lives or else they are terrible fathers. It is easy to make a single dad believe such drivel. After all, he is motivated by the guilt he still feels from the failure of his relationship that left his children in a broken home.
The problem with this is that children aren't programmed to be the center of anybody's world. They were never meant to be the number one priority. To make them such only creates tiny little monsters who believe the world revolves around them.

But I digress.

In order to effectively manage Mini-Wife Syndrome, you will need your husband on your side.

Listen up Ladies… *You cannot do this by being a Class A Bitch all the time.*

Nagging and bitching can be effective, but only if used sparingly. Did your Mama ever tell you that you can catch more flies with honey than vinegar?

It's true and it's the same in our marriages.

Look back to when you and your husband first met. Are you the same sweet woman he fell in love with? Are your words soft and sweet? Do you care about your appearance? Are you still doing the same things for him now that you did for him then? If you want your husband to change how he deals with his daughter, he has to be motivated from within. That is, he has to *want* to change in order to please his lady wife. A man might make temporary changes in response to his wife's bitching and whining. He might even pretend to change. But if you want truly motivated change, it must come from within himself.

If your marriage is truly damaged from fighting and arguing over his kids, you might have to take some time to do some repair before you start to deal with Mini-Wife Syndrome. Take time out and strengthen your relationship. Verbalize to your husband that you'd like to become close again, like you were at the beginning. Learn to control your tongue and practice keeping your halo firmly on your head when dealing with your stepdaughter.

(Might as well get used to that halo, M'Lady. It is going to be a big part of your life from now on if you want to effectively control Mini-Wife Syndrome.)

In repairing and strengthening your marriage, it is also helpful to look at some of the things your husband gets out of catering to his Mini-Wife. What's in it for him? Why is he so determined, outside of Guilty Dad Syndrome, to continue allowing his daughter to behave so inappropriately, even to the point of destroying his marriage?

If you've ever read any relationship-help books, you've probably run across the statement that while women in relationships desire more than anything to be loved and cherished, men desire *respect and admiration*. This makes perfect sense in the context of Mini-Wife Syndrome.

After all, who admires a man more than his own daughter? Who gives him the respect he desires simply due to the dynamics of the father-daughter relationship? He has many opportunities to be her hero because she is so small and needy, and in turn, she admires his strength, his wisdom, even his stature. She looks to him for support, protection, and advice.

So what does he get out of it? Only a whole lot of what he needs to feel like a man.

What we as wives need to understand is that the same instincts that husbands have toward their daughters, they also have toward their wives, and those instincts are even stronger if nurtured and given the opportunity to grow.

So while you're focusing on strengthening your marriage, you might put some effort into making certain your husband feels respected and admired by you, his wife.

The following are a few suggestions for strengthening your relationship:

Remember the woman he fell in love with. Don't lose your mystique and individuality simply because you're married. If you were interested in herbalism or hiking or pottery before you met your husband, don't let the daily grind of being a stepmother keep you from enjoying the same now. Stepmothers tend to ruminate on the negative aspects of step parenting (since there are just so many of them). It is so important to have outside hobbies and interests to keep your mind carefree and happy.

Focus on your health. Try to eat healthy and take time out for exercise. Not only will this help you better deal with the stress of step parenting, but it will keep you looking beautiful for your husband. And looks *do* matter, Ladies. Even if you're not necessarily happy with your body size or another aspect of your appearance, make the most of what you have. I think an I-Feel-Beautiful attitude is what is attractive to a husband as much as a beautiful appearance.

Choose to be happy. Be quick to smile. A husband loves a happy wife. In fact, his instinct is to try to make you happy and he is happiest when you are happy. Now, we can wreck this whole instinct by never being happy or never seeming pleased with him, in which case he will cease to care as a self-defense mechanism. If you have done this in your marriage, realize it will take some time for him to rebuild this instinct, so start now learning to smile and *choose* to be happy.

Have friends/family you can vent to. Ya know you're going to vent. One cannot simply keep all that frustration bottled inside without it eventually exploding. JUST DON'T VENT TO YOUR HUSBAND. Have a few trustworthy family members and/or friends who will listen to your frustrations. If you are not lucky enough to have someone who will listen and encourage you, then join one of the online forums. The internet is filled with stepmothers just like yourself who are going through many of the same things.

Be quick to praise your husband. If you think he's just plain sexy changing that flat tire, say it Girl! He might blush, but he will love to hear it. If you appreciate that he works hard to provide a great life for your family, no need to keep that a secret. Men love to hear praise, especially from their wives. And it is especially helpful when you can praise him as a parent. If he does something right in his parenting, tell him. It can make a world of difference.

Show your vulnerable side. A husband has very natural protective instincts toward his wife, but again, we can squelch those instincts by seeming to never need protecting. If he thinks we can take care of ourselves, he will never feel the need to step up and take care of us. Or worse, he thinks we can most certainly take care of ourselves but his poor Mini-Wife, on the other hand, needs protection *from us*. If he never sees our vulnerable side, we can easily become the Big Bad Wolf.

So, dear lady stepmother, if you've given the impression of being *too independent*, you might have a lot of repair work to do. You might start with things as simple as asking him to open a stubborn jar for you. Then you can move on to showing him your vulnerability. Let him know how it hurts you when you feel excluded. Tell him how awkward and embarrassed it makes you feel when he chooses to sit on her side of the booth instead of with you. Allow yourself to cry if you feel like it.

I know it's hard. Nowadays, we are raised to be strong, independent woman. It just feels wrong to let someone see our soft inner core. But if you want to be first in your husband's thoughts, you need to activate his instincts toward you, his wife.

Keep that HALO on your head! I know, I know… wearing a halo is soooo aggravating. It gets tarnished. It gets crooked. It falls down around your neck and threatens to become a noose. But trust me, Ladies, you neeed that halo and it would behoove you to learn to wear it well, *especially* with issues involving your stepdaughter.

And learn to control your tongue. Even if you have to hog-tie your tongue to your teeth, learn to stop bitching and nagging. Whine if you must. Go ahead and cry. BUT DON'T NAG! Husbands loathe a nagging wife.

Speak to him of your concerns in little doses and pick your battles carefully, as well as the time of the day you choose to speak to him. Don't catch him when he comes home tired and aggravated from work and begin talking to him about problems at home. Wait until he's rested and in a receptive mood to discuss anything that you know will be difficult for him.

Humor can also go a long way in helping lighten the load of day to day issues. For instance, the following transpired the day my stepdaughter decided to take my place as Daddyyy's Beer-Fetcher…

A little backstory: My husband is an active person who is in constant motion... fixing stuff around the house, fishing, caring for our farm animals or what have you. I came into the marriage with zero knowledge of any of this stuff, so I just follow him around and help in whatever way I can (and sometimes it really isn't helpful at all), making up Official Titles for myself as we go. If, for instance, "We" are building a fence, he might be the Post-Hole Digger, The Cross Brace Setter, and the Nail Gun Operator, while I am the Tool Holder, the Small Nail Hammerer, and most importantly, the BEER FETCHER. If we are fishing, he might be the Bait Hooker, the Pole Holder, and the Reelin'-Her-In-er, but I am the Fish Netter... and the Beer Fetcher!

Cause even he says I am the best Beer Fetcher he's ever seen.

It is a well-known fact to all our Facebook friends he values me as his Beer Fetcher. Shell has overheard and seen this many times from her own Facebook.

And as I was saying, Shell decided one day to take my place as Beer Fetcher...

Shell: Daddyyy, why don't you ever let me get your beer? I'm old enough, and I ain't gonna drink it.

Big D: (shrugs) Okay, well get me a beer then.

Shell: Okay, Daddyyy… (runs off happily toward the beer cooler.)

Katie: (blinking up at Big D and pushing her bottom lip out.) "If you want to replace me as your Beer-Fetcher, I understand. But I think you should know that I have much more experience and am a much better Beer-Fetcher than she is."

Big D: (looking a bit horrified.) "Of course not, Baby. You'll always be my Beer-Fetcher."

Katie: "Thank you, Baby. I love you."

Big D: (now wearing his ain't-she-cute grin) "You're welcome, Baby. I love you, too."

The very next day my daughter overheard this conversation…

Big D: "Shell, hand me a beer out of the cooler."

Shell: (throwing her hands in the air) "Yayyyy! I'm the Beer Fetcher!!!"

Big D: "No. You're not the Beer Fetcher. Katie is the Beer Fetcher. I just need you to hand me a beer cause she's not here."

Awww…. Ain't he sweet?

If I hadn't chosen my words carefully, used humor, and been willing to show my vulnerability, what *could* have transpired was this...

Shell: Daddyyy, why don't you ever let me get your beer? I'm old enough and I ain't gonna drink it.

Big D: (Shrugs) Okay, well get me a beer then.

Shell: Okay, Daddyyy... (runs off happily toward the beer cooler.)

Katie: "So now you're letting her take my place as your wife by carrying your beer to you!?!"

Big D: (Completely befuddled by this accusation because men do not understand the way women think and the issue of the Mini-Wife is especially elusive.) "What the hell are you talking about?"

Katie: "Not only do I get you a beer when you need it, I also keep the damn beer cooler stocked with beer and ice, and I drive your ass around when it is drunk. So you want a new Beer-Fetcher? Then you've got problems, Buddy, cause she can't do it like I can." (Stomp off mad, leaving him aggravated and confused.)

Shell: (Returning with the beer.) "Here ya go, Daddyyyy."

Big D: "Thank you, Baby."

Shell: "Am I your new Beeeer-Fetcherrrr???"

Big D: "Yeah, Baby, you're the new Beer Fetcher."

You see the difference? Because I remembered the halo, kept it polished, and had been working toward re-activating Big D's husbandly instincts toward me, what could have turned into a huge argument that went on for several days, not to mention left a sore spot in my heart for months, turned into a victory for me and an important lesson for Shell.

That lesson? *You cannot compete with your stepmother.* It is the same lesson she should have learned years ago when she was going through the Electra Complex stage of her development but failed to grasp. Better late than never, right? The sooner she learns she cannot compete with me, the sooner she can move on to developing in a more healthy way.

As far as Big D is concerned, he's just happy it didn't turn into a big argument, because more than anything else, men just want *peace.* It is a mistake for women to think that men always understand what they're thinking and feeling because, well, men just think differently. More than likely, when he agrees with you on this issue (and most other issues), he's just trying to figure out what makes you happy and go along with it.

The fact of the matter is, it is extremely hard for a man to understand Mini-Wife Syndrome. He does not see, or even want to see, all the little underlying cattiness going on between two people he loves. In the next chapter we are going to discuss some of the ways we can talk to our men about Mini-Wife Syndrome and some of the things we can do to help them see what is actually going on, but let me warn you... he's probably still not going to fully understand. Your best bet in controlling Mini-Wife Syndrome is in strengthening your relationship and activating his husbandly instincts towards you as much as possible so that he will make you his first priority in the home.

Helping Your Husband Understand Mini-Wife Syndrome

I was almost completely tongue-tied the first time I tried to talk to my husband about Mini-Wife Syndrome. For one thing, I didn't even have a name for it. It was very awkward trying to explain to Big D that it felt wrong to watch him and Shell cuddle and hold hands at the restaurant while I sat on the other side of the booth alone. And I could come up with no good reason for it except *that it just felt wrong*.

I told him I felt excluded. He figured I was jealous, but even though I was jealous to an extent, it was more than that. I wanted him to understand. Jealously seems so... petty and small. Something I should just be able to get over. Jealousy does not even begin to describe the negative feelings brought about by Mini-Wife Syndrome.

To make matters worse, my husband would talk about "keeping the peace" between the two of us, as if he was a polygamist who must mediate between his two wives rather than the Husband of One Wife with whom he would do better to work to get his daughter under control.

Sometimes I still don't think he "gets it." He understands there's a problem. He even understands there is a competition. But he still doesn't always recognize when it's happening, how he's being manipulated, or how he's hurt my feelings when he's inadvertently allowed her to take my place yet again.

So don't get your hopes up, Girls. If all he can understand at first is that it hurts your feelings and he's willing to put a stop to it for that reason alone, then consider it a victory. If you figure out a way to totally make him understand, then please, please, shoot me an email and share your secret.

That said, the following are some of the ways a wife might talk to her husband about Mini-Wife Syndrome in hopes that he'll "get it"…

Don't place blame. If your husband feels like you are blaming him for this elusive, abnormal Mini-Wife Syndrome, you've lost him from the get-go. You might begin by explaining that it's very common in divorced dads with daughters, and that it comes from someone trying really hard to be a good daddy but with an empty spot next to him that his daughter gradually manages to fill. Explain that it looks so very innocent that almost no one can pick up on it until the person that is supposed to fill that spot comes along and finds it is already occupied. Assure him that he's a great dad and that he's done nothing wrong. He just needs to correct the situation because it could become a major problem for the dynamics of the family.

Show him the list of symptoms of Mini-Wife Syndrome as discussed in Chapter 1. Better yet, give him my booklet, *Mini-Wife Syndrome: A Divorced Dad's Guide*, sold on www.miniwifesyndrome.com in online bookstores. Because the first step in helping your husband understand Mini-Wife Syndrome is getting him to acknowledge to himself that there is, indeed, a problem with his daughter's behavior rather than simply a problem with his wife's head. It is usually far easier for a man to accept that his daughter might have a problem if the suggestion comes from an outside source. If he is able to see for himself that his daughter has the symptoms of Mini-Wife Syndrome, you are well on your way toward correcting it.

It's good for the child to see a healthy family. You might go a little bit into the psychology behind Mini-Wife Syndrome and explain to your husband that it's healthy for his daughter to see a marriage set up the way it's meant to be. It's important for her to see her father putting his wife in the place of Queen so that his daughter can expect the same respect and concern from the man she grows up to marry.

Let him know what hurts your feelings. Like when he surprises you with flowers, but then makes it less special by surprising Mini-Wife, as well. Or when he makes you feel like less than his best friend by telling secrets, dwelling on old times, or making inside jokes with his daughter.

Make him aware of your expectations as Queen. Explain to your husband that you expect to be treated as his wife, with all the rights and privileges that go along with that, whether stepdaughter is present or not. Ask him to teach his daughter that certain rights and responsibilities are reserved for the wife in the marriage and she will no longer be allowed to cross that line.

Point out how he might feel if the roles were reversed. Remember, his greatest needs as a man in the marriage are respect and admiration. Ask him how he would feel if you took all your problems to your son rather than to your husband? What if you valued the advice of your son more than the advice of your husband? What if you admired your son's strength and wisdom more than that of your husband? He might not understand that it hurts us to feel less cherished and loved than our stepdaughter, but he might just understand if he is able to imagine how he'd feel if his greatest needs were being met for someone else rather than himself.

A picture is worth a thousand words. If you catch your husband and his Mini-Wife in an inappropriate position, take a picture and show it to him later. He might have no idea how physically developed his daughter has become, but if he sees a picture of himself looking much like a middle-aged pervert with a sweet young girlfriend, a light bulb might just go off in his head.

Point out "normal couples" in public. You know, the ones with the husband and wife holding hands and the kids following along behind. Or the ones sitting like normal human couples on one side of the booth while the daughter sits happily on the other.

Taking Your Place as Queen

So now your husband knows that Mini-Wife Syndrome exists and is a problem in his home (even if still he only thinks it is a problem in your own head). You have worked on yourself and your marriage and feel your relationship is reasonably strong enough for change. *Now* is the time for the two of you to begin working together toward helping your stepdaughter understand her proper role in the home.

In other words, it's time to take off the halo and get out the crown.

Okay, I know I'm switching channels on you here, but sometimes you've *gotta* wear the crown. After all, what good is being Queen if you never wear the crown?

The key to wearing the crown is to wear it *sparingly* so that it doesn't get old and it doesn't lose its sparkle.

That said, Your Grace... NEVER accept less than that to which you are entitled.

As women, and especially as stepmothers, we tend to bend over backwards to make others happy rather than think about ourselves. This is especially true if we've been wearing the halo too much and never bringing out the crown. Generally speaking, a man will only treat you as well as you demand to be treated. In other words, he will forget the crown exists if he hasn't seen it in a while.

That's not to say we should turn into First Class Bitches as soon as the crown comes out (though we do reserve that right to ourselves). That is only to say we should all have certain Royal Edicts that we will not allow to be crossed. We will be sweet. We will be gracious. But we will be treated as befits us as queen or we *will* rain down our wrath as only a queen is wont to do.

Every stepmother should put some thought into her own personal Royal Edicts. What does it mean for you to be Queen? What are your rights in the home and in your marriage?

The following are some examples of a few (but not all) of the Royal Edicts I have declared. Perhaps some of them will not seem as important to you as they are to me. Some of them might even seem petty to you. That's why it is important for you to put some thought into the things that will make you happy in your own relationship.

I retain the sole right to be my husband's Best Friend. We had a magical first year of our relationship. Unfortunately, it was often marred by the every other weekend visits with his daughter, during which time I was relegated to Second Best Friend. I thought I could live with it at the time, but as the honeymoon wore off, this issue simultaneously became more pronounced on their part and less able to tolerate on my part, until we arrived at a crossroads and an ultimatum: He will treat me the same, whether Shell is present or not. Otherwise, I would spend every other weekend elsewhere. He chose to keep me around.

I have the right to the majority of my husband's physical affection. Sure, it is normal for a father to show affection toward his child; however, if I am forever sitting around watching the two of them cuddle, hold hands, hug, kiss, etc., then that is definitely NOT normal. It is also abnormal for a man to worry what his daughter will think of him showing his wife physical affection, yet many a father with a Mini-Wife feels awkward hugging and kissing his wife in front of his daughter because he knows it will make her jealous. Big D had to learn that the problem was not with him showing affection toward his wife. It was his daughter's inappropriate response to it.

I have the right to sit next to my husband. Furthermore, I have the right to hold his hand and walk next to him in public. This was one of the hardest things for my husband to deal with because in public is where Shell seemed to cling to him most. We had some ugly first few times in restaurants when my husband chose to sit next to me instead of Shell. She pouted the entire time. Then he got it in his silly head I was going to take turns with Shell, with him alternately sitting on my side then sitting on hers. Um…NO. He learned that unfortunate fact after I left him sitting in the restaurant looking pretty stupid cuddling with his Mini-Wife daughter opposite a vacant booth.

I am Baby. She is not. I got pretty tired of trying to figure out who my husband was addressing when he began a sentence with, "Baby, would you…" Shell was determined he was always talking to her. But since he had called me "Baby" from the beginning of our relationship and it was my favorite of his nicknames for me, I had to insist he stop calling her "Baby" and make it plain who owned the Baby pet name (me).

I am my husband's helper. As I mentioned before, my husband is very handy around the house. Much of our time is spent with my husband working on a project and me following him around making up jobs (along with appropriate job titles) for myself. When my step-daughter came to live with us, she decided she was going to be Daddy's helper, and competed with me ad nauseum to take care of his every need. We are still fighting this battle, but Big D is very aware and sensitive to my desire to be his helpmate so it is rarely a problem for us.

My husband and I are on the same team. I am never a Happy Queen if I am made to feel like the outsider. This includes joking around. My stepdaughter is a master at catching my husband unawares and jumping onto a team with him. They are on the Fried Fish team simply because I baked fish one night. They are on the Chicken Gizzard team because I don't like them. They are on the Poor-Mistreated, No-Clean-Socks Team if I haven't done laundry. You get the picture. I have asked my husband to please speak to me in private if he has complaints or issues with me to prevent this Jumping-onto-His-Team-Unawares Issue. He has gotten much better at staying on Our

Team and defusing any notion that he is on any Other Team.

I retain the sole right to go on dates with my husband. I know this one is controversial -- that many people believe a man should have Dadddyyy-Daughterrrr time with his Mini-Wife -- but I strongly disagree. In fact, to give the Mini-Wife dates with her father not only reinforces her belief that she is equal in status to her stepmother, but also gives birth to more competition between the two as to whom gets to go on the most dates, the funnest dates, the most expensive dates, etc. In our household, we only have two options for going out... dates between my husband and myself, and outings for the whole family that includes my husband and I, my daughter, and his daughter.

I will decorate my castle... er... house... however I wish. If I was to feel at home in my house, I felt I needed the right to decorate and make changes as I pleased. Since it was Big D's house before I moved in, Shell had a problem with some of the changes I made, even though my husband had told me he didn't care if I nailed up Corn Flake boxes on the walls as long as I didn't remove his deer horns from the wall. I took him at his word. The deer horns remain, but everything else is fair game.

Dealing with Mini-Wife Syndrome
Along with Your Husband

It would seem that your husband would have the biggest role in dealing with Mini-Wife Syndrome, but generally that is not the case. The fact of the matter is, he is probably going to have the smallest role and make the smallest effort to correct the problem.

Why? Number one, because he is going to be the one least likely to see there is a problem, and if he does see there is a problem, he's going to be the one least negatively affected by it. Number two, he still carries all that guilt that makes it feel "wrong" to him to make his daughter unhappy, so correcting the problem (i.e. making her unhappy) is going to be very difficult for him.

So you see, dear stepmother, the bulk of controlling this disease lies with us. Not only do we have to be consistent in teaching the Mini-Wife from our end that she is not the wife, we have to continue to encourage and advise our husbands on how to correct Mini-Wife Syndrome from his position as Daddyyyy. This can become frustrating and discouraging and make it more important than ever to take care of ourselves both physically and mentally.

However, the following are some of the things you might do to help your husband stay focused on controlling/correcting Mini-Wife Syndrome…

Give him some time to correct the problem. If you require him to make all the changes at once, he is going to feel like his daughter is being mistreated and his protective instincts toward her will be kicked into full gear. This is counterproductive to your cause. Explain to him that you understand this has been going on for quite some time and some of the changes may have to be gradual.

Stay positive and on his team. If he thinks you are doing all of this to hurt his precious princess, he is going to resist, but if he understands you are truly doing what is best for his daughter, he will be more cooperative in correcting it. Remind him often that Mini-Wife Syndrome is ultimately as bad for the Mini-Wife as it is for the stepmother. Remind him that his daughter needs to see a happy, healthy marriage so that she can strive for a similarly healthy marriage when she chooses a mate. Be positive and encourage him to be kind to his daughter in other ways that don't involve her taking your place as wife.

Fiercely guard your job as wife. Let your husband know frequently (completely separate and apart from any conversation about the Mini-Wife) how much you value being his helpmate. Tell him YOU want to be the one taking care of him because that's your job as his wife. Then if he allows her to horn in on your job, he will understand why your feelings are hurt. And do let him know, in your angelic sort of way, that your feelings are hurt. Hopefully soon you will find him protecting your position as wife every bit as much as you do.

Consider counseling for your stepdaughter. Change is difficult and this is going to be a big change for her. Talk to your husband about getting a qualified counselor on board to help your stepdaughter get on track toward more normal psychological development.

Devise a plan together. Begin by making a list of all the symptoms of Mini-Wife Syndrome that your stepdaughter is exhibiting (and be willing to add to and revise the list as time goes on.) Then prioritize which symptoms are most troublesome and brainstorm things he might do to correct the problem with the least disruption to his daughter. Set goals with your husband based on the list and interventions. Keep an open discussion about what goals you are working on at any given time so he continues to keep working toward correcting the problem.

A sample plan for my 12 year old stepdaughter might read as follows:

Problem #1: Shell is overly affectionate with her father, even to the point of being inappropriate.

Goal: Big D will gradually withdraw from excessive physical affection with Stepdaughter.

Interventions:

1. Big D will withdraw from hugs after one second

2. Big D will no longer kiss stepdaughter on the lips. He will explain to her that it is no longer appropriate since she is growing into a young lady.

3. Big D will limit hugs/kisses with his daughter to just before leaving for work in the morning and just before going to bed at night, unless there is another legitimate reason for physical affection.

Problem #2: Shell becomes upset when Big D shows physical affection to Katie Lee.

Goal: Shell will learn to accept physical affection between Big D and Katie Lee and recognize that it is part of a healthy marriage.

Interventions:

1. Big D will explain to Shell that Katie Lee is his wife and husbands and wives are supposed to show physical affection to one another.

2. Big D will not limit physical affection to Katie Lee in the presence of his daughter.

3. Big D will provide at least double the amount of physical affection for Katie Lee than he does for his daughter.

Problem #3: Shell begs to go on private dates with Big D

Goal: Remove the potential for competition over Big D's time.

Interventions:

1. Big D will not go on private dates with Shell.

2. Big D will explain to Shell that private dates in our families are only for couples, in our case, Big D. and Katie Lee. All other dates will be family dates including Big D., Katie Lee, Katie Lee's daughter, and Shell.

Problem #4: Shell pouts and becomes angry if she is not the center of attention.

Goal: Do not reward bad behavior with attention.

Interventions:

1. Big D will pretend not to notice if Shell is pouting.

2. Big D will discipline Shell for angry outbursts by

putting her in timeout away from the family. He will do this with the least discussion possible (i.e. negative attention).

3. Big D and Katie Lee will reward Shell with positive attention for good behavior.

Problem #5: Shell tries to "team up" with Big D against Katie Lee whenever possible.

Goal: Big D and Katie Lee will remain a solid united front.

Interventions:

1. Big D will speak privately with Katie Lee of any concerns he has involving Katie Lee.

2. If Big D inadvertently opens the door for Shell to jump onto his team against Katie Lee, he will immediately make it clear he and Katie Lee are a united front.

3. Big D will never, even in play, pick on Katie Lee in the presence of Shell.

The advantage to making a *written* plan with your husband's input is that he is fully aware and acknowledges that each of the problems exist and he has input into and full knowledge of what he is expected to do about it. (However, if your husband is not the type to do a written plan or a verbal plan is as far as you can get with him, then by all means make a verbal plan.) Be as detailed and clear in your plan as possible, and be open and willing to include positive interventions, as well. As long as you seem like you want what's best not only for your marriage but also for your stepdaughter, your husband will be more likely to participate in setting these goals and interventions.

Dealing with Mini-Wife Syndrome when Your Husband Won't

Sometimes, despite all your talks, your frustration with the situation, all your begging and pleading for your husband to do something, anything, about Mini-Wife Syndrome, he will refuse to act. This is, in fact, very common. Whether he is in denial or he simply cannot overcome the Guilty Dad Syndrome that causes him to ignore such inappropriate behavior, don't be surprised if your husband just doesn't deal with Mini-Wife Syndrome at all.

In this case, dear stepmother, you MUST learn to guard your mental health. Mini-Wife Syndrome is very hard on a wife who loves her husband and if left unchecked, can lead to anxiety, depression, personality changes, PTSD symptoms, even physical illness.

A big part of the problem is feeling as if you have no "safe haven" in your own home. This constant stress, lack of comfort, and feeling of emptiness is what I refer to as "emotional homelessness." It is when you start to feel like an outcast in your own home.

The first thing I would recommend is **creating yourself a haven somewhere in your home.** This might be your bedroom, a spare room, a she-shed, the attic, even a closet if it is large enough… make yourself a comfortable nest where Mini-Wife is NOT permitted to intrude… A place where you can go for a break, a cup of coffee or wine, and just breathe and feel free from the Mini-Wife situation for a time… and take as much time away as you need.

Which brings me to my second point. **You do NOT have to participate in a situation that makes you desperately unhappy.** Remove yourself from the Mini-Wife triangle if need be. If they are cuddling on the couch, leave the room. They're walking hand in hand in the store? There's no law that says you must follow meekly behind. Just walk away. Refuse to sit opposite of them in the restaurant while they behave like teenage lovers.

And if Mini-Wife is permitted to interrupt your adult conversations whenever she pleases, the conversation ends there. Leave him wondering what you were about to say before Mini-Wife abruptly ended your sentence.

Become comfortable "speaking up" whenever Mini-Wife is breaking the rules or is misbehaving. Sometimes all your husband needs is a little nudge or reminder that he needs to be noticing and correcting these things.

Learn the art of disengagement, go out with friends and do your own thing while the mini-wife is present. (Please note: I am NOT suggesting you be unfaithful to your husband.) Be honest and up-front with your husband and let him know why you are disengaging and enjoying life without him. Make sure he is aware he has broken the marriage covenant by putting another in your place.

If you are actually FINANCING the Daddy-Mini-Wife dynamic then STOP. You have no obligation to put your money toward something that makes you so unhappy.

You have no obligation to cater to the Mini-Wife just because your husband does or because either of them demand it. You have the right to take your own children out for a treat, make whatever you'd like for dinner, and prioritize your own needs first with whatever resources you have available.

And above all, **STOP RUMINATING!** Limit the amount of time you allow Mini-Wife to occupy your thoughts. Focus on making your life happy for yourself. Practice being kind to yourself and taking good care of your body, mind, and spirit.

Finally, consider counseling… either for yourself or for the two of you as a couple, but be selective as to the therapist you choose as some can be very unsympathetic towards stepmothers.

CONCLUSION

As you can see, much of what you can do to contain Mini-Wife Syndrome revolves around teaching the Mini-Wife that she cannot take your place, she does not have the power of an adult, and she should not even try to compete with you. Only then can the Mini-Wife start to move along with more normal development (and if she does not, please consider taking her to a qualified counselor.)

I'm not going to lie to you. Controlling Mini-Wife Syndrome is not easy. It takes time and thought and effort that you might resent since you did not create the problem to begin with. But as I've said before, somewhere around 75% of our marriages end in divorce.

Is your marriage worth it?

Mine is.

DON'T MISS IT!!!

The companion guide to
Mini-Wife Syndrome: A Stepmother's Guide
is now available in online bookstores!!!

Mini-Wife Syndrome:
A Divorced Dad's Guide

Made in United States
Troutdale, OR
10/31/2024